FIRST PRINCIPLES

OF THE DOCTRINES

OF CHRIST

PIETER VAN STADEN

MoB
MESSENGERS OF BLESSING

Enquiries can be made by email to: pieter@mweb.co.za.

ISBN 978-0-620-61887-8

Introduction

Hebrews 6:1-2 lists the elementary teachings about Christ. In Assemblies of God circles they have been known as the First Principles. This booklet can be used to teach them in eight lessons under the headings outlined in the Contents.

The lessons follow a natural progression. They relate in chronological order to events believers experience. Chapters 1 and 2 have to do with salvation, 3-6 are about our walk with God while 7 & 8 are concerned with the next life.

The lessons are are by no means exhaustive. Controversial subjects have been excluded in this introductory course. Discussions about the intermediate state of the dead, the the great tribulation or the timing of the rapture should best be avoided. The class should preferably be taught by someone who is well versed in the Bible and able to answer difficult questions. The doctrines can be made more relevant to learners by examples from the teacher's own experience.

It needs to be emphasised that the lessons are about Christ. Those attending these sessions are assumed to have had some experience of the living Christ, or at least to believe that Jesus is the Son of God. Seekers who do not as yet have that confidence might do better by first investigating the reliability of the Bible and the claims of Jesus.

Contents

1.

Repentance from dead works

According to the Analytical Greek Lexicon, the word used in the Bible for repentance, *metanoia*, means change of mode of thought and feeling, making a change of principle and of practice. In other words, think and act differently!

> As soon as you discover
> that you are going
> in the wrong direction,
> just turn around
> and you will be facing
> the right direction.
>
> GLEN A McQUIRK

When reading our Bible we may question why John the Baptist preached a *baptism of repentance* (Mark 1:4). And why Jesus started his three years of preaching with the words: "The kingdom of God has come near. *Repent and believe the good news!*" (Mark 1:15). Also, we may wonder why Jesus' last conversation with the apostles included the words "...and *repentance for the forgiveness of sins* will be preached in his name to all nations ..." (Luke 24:47).

The answer, looked at **from God's perspective**, is that he wants us to know how different he is from us. In the Bible this is referred to as the *holiness* of God. We have proof of it in the form of his commands and actions. After Adam and Eve had sinned, God drove them out from his presence. No human was allowed in his company. They had to approach God with animal sacrifices, indicating that they agreed with the Lord about their sinfulness. They accepted that blood had to be shed for their sins to be forgiven.

Centuries later the Lord told the Israelites to build a tent (the tabernacle), and later still, Solomon built a temple. Inside the temple was the Holy Place. A portion of it, the Holy of Holies, was separated by a thick curtain from the rest of the Holy Place. It served as a reminder to them that they could not see God and live.

- Can you think of other examples in the Bible and Jewish culture which point to the fact that God is holy?

The status of mankind was drastically changed when Jesus became human, lived a perfect life, and paid the ultimate penalty by dying for our sins. This ransom payment was accepted in heaven. We know that for sure because God raised Jesus from the dead to sit at his right hand (Hebrews 1:3).

> There is now a human being in God's presence in heaven.

From a human point of view we get to understand the need for repentance when we reflect on the motives which drive the *natural human being*. Paul maintained that the *soul person*, (*psychikos* in Greek) "does not accept the things that come from the Spirit of God" (1 Corinthians 2:14). We find ourselves in a dilemma when we decide to live for the glory of God. Up to that time our minds have been trained to ask: *What's in it for me?* Our eyes have become used to look at people and things in ways which offend God. Our habits have formed pathways in our brains which determine our *reflex actions*.

In the light of the above, sinners cannot please God by tweaking their lives with New Year resolutions, or by re-forming or reinventing themselves. God insists that we get rid of our old way of thinking; *our minds must be transformed* (Romans 12.2).

When we realise how disrespectful we have been to God, our *feelings* should not be untouched. Peter cried bitterly after he had denied the Lord three times (Luke 22:62). Afterwards he challenged the crowd that gathered on the day of Pentecost and they were *"cut to the heart"* (Acts 2:37). God will not despise a heart which is broken and sorrowful (Psalm 51:17). When we enter into the new covenant, God puts his laws in our hearts (Hebrews 10:16).

Though mind and feelings play a role in the process of repentance, a more important aspect of a person's being that must be engaged, is one's *will*. Salespeople talk about *buyer's regret*. That is when we buy something on impulse and later berate ourselves for acquiring it.

> A man convinced against his will is of the same opinion still.

- Can you remember an occasion when you were convinced against your will, or when you noticed how someone else reverted back to his/her original opinion?

Giving mental assent to the truth of the gospel, agreeing that Jesus died for our sin, is not enough. Nor is having an emotional experience after hearing the good news. There must be a willingness to *obey* the gospel which implies a *change in behaviour.*

- What changed in your life when you trusted Jesus to save you, and what is still changing?

Dead works can in the first place refer to evil deeds. The *works of the flesh* are described in Galatians 5:19. "Flesh" in this context denotes the evil nature of man without God. People say: To sleep with my girlfriend/boyfriend is *natural.* Repentance involves killing natural passions "which wage war against your soul" (1 Peter 2:11). Jesus said: "it is from within, out of a person's heart, that evil thoughts come" (Mark 7:21). He proceeded to list the sins which originate in the heart. A shorter list is found in Matthew 15:19. Combined the lists comprise murders, adulteries, sexual immorality (fornications, *porneiai* in Greek), thefts, false testimonies, slander (blasphemy), greediness, vices, deceit, licentiousness (outrageous behaviour), envy (evil eye), arrogance, foolishness. He used drastic terms to warn his followers of the danger of sin. Plucking out your right eye or cutting off your right hand or foot, if they cause you to sin, is better for you than to be cast into the eternal fire (Matthew 5:29-30; 18:8-10).

The Ten Commandments were given to make us human beings aware of our sinful nature (Romans 3:20; 7:7). Paul warned against sinful behaviour in each of his letters. He spoke about God's anger because of it. The verses in the various letters are in: Romans 1:18-32, 1 Corinthians 6:9-11, 2 Corinthians 11:13-15, Galatians 5:19-21, Ephesians 5:5, Philippians 3:18-19, Colossians 3:5-6, 1 Thessalonians 4:3-6, 2 Thessalonians 2:9-12, 1 Timothy 1:9-10, 2 Timothy 3:1-5, Titus 1:10-12.

Dead works can also be understood to be works done by people *dead to God*. Someone who has not received Christ is separated from God and spiritually dead. (Ephesians 2:1). Many people think their religious deeds will put them in God's good books. Cain was such a person. Abel, on the other hand, killed an innocent animal to pay for his sin. Cain was cross because God did not accept his offering which represented his "good deeds". Just like a dead person cannot do anything at all, an unregenerate person cannot please God (Romans 8:8). *We must come to God on his terms.* "...he is patient with you, not wanting anyone to perish, but everyone to come to repentance" (2 Peter 3:9).

The Holy Spirit is at work when someone repents; it is he who makes a person aware of the sin of not believing in Jesus (John 16:8). The Father is also involved; no-one can come to Jesus unless the Father draws him (John 6:44). Our duty is to turn around; *God regenerates us.* Jesus told Nicodemus that unless a person is born from above he/she cannot see God's kingdom (John 3:3).

2.

Faith toward God

Faith is: regarding what is hoped for, the *assurance;* and the *proof* of things not seen (Hebrews 11:1, PvS).

Faith has an *object*; that means it is directed at someone or something; a Christian's faith is directed at Jesus and God.

Jesus said that whoever does not receive the kingdom of God like a little child, will never enter it (Mark 10:15).

By studying the numerous passages in the Bible that deal with faith it is possible to identify at least three kinds.

a) Saving faith. Since "all have sinned" (Romans 3:23) we should all be found guilty in the law court of heaven. Paul wrote a letter to the Galatians to convince them to "know that a person is not justified by the works of the law, but by faith in Jesus Christ. So we, too, have put our faith in Christ Jesus that we may be justified by faith in Christ and not by the works of the law, because

> The word **"justified"** is a legal term which means **"not guilty"**.

by the works of the law no one will be justified." He added "I do not set aside the grace of God, for if righteousness could be gained through the law, Christ died for nothing!" (Galatians 2:16, 21).

- What are the two ways Paul mentioned by which people attempt to get right with God?

- What was Paul's reason for saying there is only one way in which we can be justified?

Abraham is regarded as the father of our faith because, like Abraham, we are justified by faith. "Abram believed the Lord, and he credited it to him as righteousness" (Genesis 15:6).

To be reckoned righteous means the same as to be justified or to be declared innocent and blameless.

According to John 3:36 in the NLT, believing in the Son is the opposite of disobeying him. The word *disobey* can also be translated *defy, reject* or *refuse to comply*. The *wrath (angry judgement)* of God remains on everyone who does not believe in the Son.

You're gonna have to
serve somebody,
Well, it may be the devil
or it may be the Lord
But you're gonna have to
serve somebody.

BOB DYLAN

According to James 2:17 faith without works is dead. This verse was abused by the church during the Middle Ages. People were promised forgiveness of sins in exchange for good works. In 1517 Martin Luther's opposition to this custom and to other malpractices in the Roman Catholic Church initiated the Reformation in Germany. He claimed that salvation could not be obtained through good works, but by faith alone. One of his favourite sayings was: *The just shall live by faith.* This sentence is found in Habakkuk 2:4 and repeated 3 times in the New Testament. This faith is a free gift from God, not something we can work for, but we are saved to do good works which God prepared in advance for us to do (Ephesians 2:8-10).

> We are saved by faith alone but saving faith never stays alone.

b) Miracle working faith. Jesus said: "If you have faith as a mustard seed, you can say to this mountain 'Move from here to there' and it will move" (Matthew 17:20). He repeated this truth: "... if you have faith and do not doubt ... and if you say to this mountain 'Be thrown into the sea', it will be done" (Matthew 21:21).

The Jews asked Jesus: "What must we do to do the works God requires?" Jesus answered, "The work of God is this: to believe in the one he has sent" (John 6:29).

Faith (of the mountain moving kind) is a *gift of the Holy Spirit* (1 Corinthians 12:7-9). George Muller (1805-1898) is often quoted as one who had extraordinary faith. He received more than one and a half million pounds sterling in answer to prayer during his lifetime, housing and feeding almost 10 000 orphans.

The Bible contains many accounts of miracles. Each one of them required above average faith. Imagine taking 120 years to build a ship, going to an unknown country or healing a cripple. Since they defy natural laws the majority of people don't believe these stories, or regard them as fables. However, we believe God designed the laws of nature. Therefore we can accept that he can override nature's laws.

Hall of Fame of Faith Heroes.

Hebrews 11

c) Faithfulness. God has assigned each believer with an amount of faith, enough to exercise his/her gifts (natural and spiritual) (Romans 12:3). For example, those who have the gift of prophesy should use it in proportion to their faith (Romans 12:6). Jesus illustrated this truth by telling a parable of a man who entrusted his servants with money for them to do business with. He expected them to increase the amount they received (Matthew 25:14-30).

When the apostles asked Jesus to increase their faith, he told them a parable about faithfulness (Luke 17:5-10). Later he told his disciples a parable to show them that they should *always pray and not give up* (Luke 18:1-8).

- Is *giving up* the same as *suffering from depression?*

- What is the most common remedy for depression?

- Do you think someone who is depressed should ask the elders to pray for him/her (James 5:13-14)?

Our faith will be tested. We must consider it pure joy when this happens because it develops perseverance and proves that our faith is genuine (James 1:2-3; 1 Peter 1:6-7). Those who believe the promises they receive from God, will be rewarded (Hebrews 11:6). If we are filled with unbelief we must not expect to receive anything from God (James 1:7). Children of God who do not expect their Heavenly Father to give them what is best for them, are insulting him (Hebrews 3:12-4:2). When we are faced with the attraction of sin we must remember that God never allows us to be tempted beyond what we can take (1 Corinthians 10:13).

- Discuss the statement: "A Christian is someone who believes God is good".

d) Hindrances to faith.

- In Mark 11:23-25 Jesus followed up his statement about moving a mountain with: "And when you stand praying, if you hold anything against anyone, forgive them...". Compare this with Ps 66:18: "If I had cherished sin in my heart, the Lord would not have listened".

- What do you think hindered the disciples' faith while Jesus was sleeping in the boat during the storm (Mark 4:40)?

- Why do you think the people in Nazareth lacked faith (Matthew 13:54-58)? In which way did their attitudes differ from those of the centurion (Matthew 8:5-13) and the Canaanite woman (Matthew 15:21-28)?

- Jesus often used the term *little faith* to describe the disciples' lack of faith (Matthew 6:30; 8:26; 13:58; 14:31; 16:8; 17:20). Why do you think he did so?

- "And now these three remain: faith, hope and love." (1 Corinthians 13:13). Until when do they remain?

3.

Baptism into Christ and in water

Four kinds of baptism are found in the Bible. The key words that identify them are **by** and **in**.

a) Baptism *by* the Holy Spirit *into* the Body of Christ. This happens when someone repents and is born again. Jesus said that unless one is born of the Spirit one cannot enter the kingdom of God (John 3:5).

The phrases "by one Spirit we were all baptised into one body" (1 Corinthians 12:13) and "baptised into Christ" (Galatians 3:27) refer to what happened when you put your faith in Jesus to save you from your sins. In a spiritual sense you became connected to all other believers. In the kingdom of God the distinctions of race, occupation and gender are abolished (Galatians 3:28). "If anyone is in Christ, the new creation has come: The old has gone, the new is here!" (2 Corinthians 5:17). The work of the Spirit is mysterious like the wind which we cannot see (John 3:8). But we can see effect of the wind and similarly a changed life is evidence of the new birth.

b) Baptism *by* a believer *in* water. The last words of Jesus to his apostles, according to Matthew, contain instructions known as the *great commission* (Matthew 28:19-20).

- What are the four instructions in the great commission?

Baptism was not foreign to the Jewish community of Jesus' day. It is practised by Jews to this day. A *mikvah* is a special bath used for ritual cleansing, based on orthodox Jewish interpretation of Old Testament verses. One of the rituals a convert to Judaism must perform, is to be immersed in a mikvah.

Jesus was baptised by his relative John in the Jordan River "to fulfil all righteousness" (Matthew 3:15). He did not need to repent, but by this act he identified with sinners, agreeing to suffer the punishment we so justly deserve (Galatians 3:13). The way in which high priests[†] of Israel were consecrated (set apart as holy), was to be washed and anointed (have oil poured on their heads) (Exodus 29:4-7). John *"washed"* Jesus but did not anoint him. However, the Father approved and anointed Jesus with the Holy Spirit, declaring from heaven: "You are my Son, whom I love; with you I am well pleased" (Mark 1:11).

[†] John was the son of the priest Zechariah and the transaction in the river may be interpreted to be Jesus' consecration as high priest (Hebrews 7:27).

New converts were baptised by Jesus (John 3:22) and the early church (Acts 2:41). It is one of the *two ordinances* the Lord *commanded* his followers to practise. The other one is Holy Communion, also known as the Breaking of Bread. Believers who want to live in obedience should therefore be baptised and break bread with other believers.

Baptism should be *public* because by submitting to it the candidates declare their allegiance to Jesus. Going under the water symbolises the death we deserve for our sin. It also indicates that we have given up the right to live for ourselves (2 Corinthians 5:15). Rising up out of the water denotes the new life we have received from Christ. By getting baptised I therefore identify with Jesus' death and resurrection and *"act"* it out for the world to see.

The Greek word *baptizo* means to dip or immerse or cleanse by washing. The first king to authorise the translation of the Bible into English was James 1 in 1611. One may ask why they did not translate *baptizo* into a common English word such as *dip, immerse* or *dunk*. Some claim that *baptise* was *fabricated* by the translators of the Bible at the insistence of King James. The king's motive had to do with the fact that he and all his subjects had only been sprinkled. If dunking had been the correct *mode of baptism,* everybody might have needed to be re-baptised.

- What do you conclude from Matthew 3:16, John 3:23 and Acts 8:38 regarding the mode of baptism?

Infants are baptised in many churches and sects, whether by sprinkling or full immersion, as practised by the Greek Orthodox Church. Infant baptism is justified by complex interpretations of difficult to understand verses. One of the stronger arguments in favour of infant baptism is that it came in the place of circumcision as a *"sign of the covenant"*. Abraham was circumcised as a grown man, so the line of reasoning goes, but his children on the eighth day.

They maintain that baptism is the sign of the *new covenant*. According to this dogma unbelievers who have not been baptised are outside of the covenant. When they come to faith they should be baptised before allowed to become members of the church. Children of people of the covenant are then to be baptised as babies. When they reach the age of understanding, their churches require them to *"confirm"* the faith their parents had exercised on their behalf.

Proponents of this point of view need to explain why all the Jewish converts, like the apostles, who were already circumcised, needed to be baptised. Also, the early church was embroiled in a dispute concerning circumcision of the non-Jewish converts (Acts 15:5-29). They need to explain why none of the apostles ended the controversy by saying:

"Baptism has taken the place of circumcision"? Instead, the apostles said: "It seemed good to the Holy Spirit and to us not to burden you with anything beyond the following ..."

- What do you think the apostles meant by "the Holy Spirit and us" in Acts 15:28?

Over the last 20 centuries promoters of *believers baptism* have been vilified, and those who practised it persecuted by the state churches of Europe and Britain. Some of the clergy in these churches believed that one was born again by the act of baptism. To withhold baptism from an infant was therefore considered a sin. Advocates of this belief have difficulty in explaining how the criminal on the cross could have been saved (Luke 23:43).

One of the verses used to bolster *baptismal regeneration*, is 1 Peter 3:21. It contains the phrase: "baptism that now saves you". However, the rest of the verse explains its meaning: "not the putting away of the filth of the flesh, but the answer of a good conscience toward God" (KJV). If you know God expects you to be baptised and then do it, your conscience will be clear regarding baptism. Your sin is not washed away by the waters of baptism but by the blood of Jesus (1 John 1:7; Revelation 1:5).

> We don't get baptised **to be** saved.
> We get baptised because **we are** saved.

- How old do you think a person should should be before he/she may be baptised?

There is a modern day aberration which states that a believer must be baptised *"in the name of Jesus"*. This teaching, often referred to as *"Jesus only"*, is a modern version of an ancient heresy which denied the doctrine of the triune God. Rather than entering into a dispute about the Trinity, this practice can be refuted by quoting the *formula* for baptism given in Matthew 28:19.

- Paul found out that certain disciples had not heard of the Holy Spirit (Acts 19:2). What did he ask them after he realised that they did not even know there was a Holy Spirit? Why do you think he asked that question?

- Comment on Luke 7:29-30: "All the people, even the tax collectors, when they heard Jesus' words, acknowledged that God's way was right, because they had been baptised by John. But the Pharisees and the experts in the law rejected God's purpose for themselves, because they had not been baptised by John."

4.

Baptism in the Holy Spirit

John the Baptist said: "I baptise you with water. But one who is more powerful than I will come, ... He will baptise you with the Holy Spirit and fire" (Luke 3:16).

c) Baptism *by* Jesus *in* the Holy Spirit. All believers have *an experience* of the Holy Spirit because he is the one who convicted us of our sin (John 16:8). No-one can be saved without having acknowledged his/her need of forgiveness. Blasphemy against the Holy Spirit is the unforgivable sin (Luke 12:10) because a person who refuses to admit his/her sin cannot be saved.

After the last supper, shortly before he was arrested, Jesus told the eleven that *the Father would give them another Comforter* (Counsellor, Advocate), seeing that he would be leaving them (John 14:16). The apostles already knew the Spirit, he said, because he had been *with* them and would later be *in* them. *"The world cannot receive him"* (John 14:17 NLT). Since I was of the world before I was born again, I could not receive him when I repented; I received Jesus.

- How do you understand the Holy Spirit to have been *with* the apostles?

After his resurrection Jesus told the disciples not to leave Jerusalem but to wait until they were baptised in the Holy Spirit (Acts 1:4-5). "You will receive power when the Holy Spirit comes on you", he said (Acts 1:8). On the day of Pentecost they were all "filled with the Holy Spirit and began to speak in other tongues as the Spirit enabled them" (Acts 2:4).

The baptism in the Holy Spirit is an experience *every believer* should seek *after conversion*. This was the case with the newly converted Samaritans. Philip went on an evangelistic campaign to Samaria and people were delivered from demons, healed, saved and baptised (Acts 8:5-8,12). Nevertheless Peter and John were sent from Jerusalem to pray for them "that they might receive the Holy Spirit." (Acts 8:14-17). Something visible must have happened when Peter and John laid hands on them because Simon the Sorcerer "saw that the Spirit was given at the laying on of the apostles' hands" (Acts 8:18).

- What do you think Simon saw when people received the Holy Spirit?

Saul of Tarsus received the Holy Spirit three days after he had seen a vision of Jesus and had repented on his way to Damascus. This happened when a disciple named Ananias laid hands on him. After this, Saul regained his sight and was baptised (Acts 9:17-18).

- In the light of 1 Corinthians 14:18, do you think there was a manifestation of the Holy Spirit through Paul when he was filled?

The centurion Cornelius was a God-fearing gentile who had a vision in which an angel told him to send men to bring Peter (Acts 10:3-5). Peter needed a vision and a voice speaking to him twice before he was willing to set foot in the house of a non-Jew (Acts 10:28). While Peter explained the good news of Jesus to Cornelius and his family and friends, they started speaking in tongues. Peter and the Jewish believers who came with him took that as *evidence* that they had received the Holy Spirit. He therefore "ordered that they be baptised" in water (Acts 10:45-48).

This account indicates that there does not have to be a time lag between accepting the message of salvation and being baptised in the Spirit. Like Saul, these people were filled with the Holy Spirit before they were even baptised in water (Acts 10:48).

- What was the first question Paul asked the group of disciples he met in Ephesus? (Acts 19:2)

- Why do you think Paul asked this question?

- What *happened* to these believers when Paul placed his hands on them? (Acts 19:6)

- What did *they do* then?

On the day of Pentecost Peter explained to the crowd what they had just witnessed:

First he insisted that "this is that" which Joel had prophesied about, namely that God would pour out his Spirit "on all people" (Acts 2:17). **Secondly**, he proclaimed the death and resurrection of Jesus. "Exalted to the right hand of God, he has received from the Father the promised Holy Spirit and has poured out what you now see and hear" (Acts 2:33; see also John 7:39).

If this is not that,
then what is this?
But if this is that,
then that's that.

The third point Peter made in his sermon, after his hearers were "cut to the heart", was to say to them "repent and be baptised ... for the forgiveness of your sins". He added that the gift of the Holy Spirit was promised to "all whom the Lord our God will call" (Acts 2:38-39).

Spirit baptism and tongue speaking have occurred in isolated places since that first day. In 1906, in a small wooden structure in Azusa Street, Los Angeles, history was made which reverberated throughout the world. People came from far and wide to experience this *"new"* phenomenon and by 1907 the Pentecostal Movement was well established in America, Britain and Europe. New churches were brought into being because most established churches opposed the doctrine of a *"second blessing"*.

In the latter part of the 20th century, especially in the seventies, thousands of the members of the traditional churches were filled with the Holy Spirit. It became known as the *Charismatic Movement*. Many books were written on the subject, such as *When the Spirit Comes* by Colin Urquhart who was an Anglican priest. Pentecostal and Charismatic churches are among the fastest growing religious organisations in the world.

For anyone who desires to receive the gift of the Holy Spirit the following points are worth considering:

1) Our heavenly Father is *more than willing* to give us the Holy Spirit (Luke 11:13).
2) We *cannot deserve* the Spirit by anything we do since he is given as a Gift.

3) The best *motive* we can have for desiring to be filled is so that we would have power to witness (Acts 1:8).

4) We have the *opportunity* to receive him every day since the Holy Spirit has been poured out and we do not have to wait.

5) The most common *means* by which believers received the gift of the Spirit in the book of Acts was by the laying on of hands.

6) The Spirit *enables* us to speak in tongues but *we do the speaking.*

7) It is *by faith* we know we are speaking words given by the Holy Spirit and not anything else (Luke 11:13).

8) Jesus likened the experience of receiving the Spirit to drinking. It would be like *"rivers of living water flowing out of your belly"* (John 7:37-38 PvS).

9) Paul explained that when one speaks in tongues, one's *mind is unfruitful* (1 Corinthians 14:14).

10) Speaking in tongues is probably one of the best ways in which a believer can practise how to *cooperate* with God the Holy Spirit.

5.

Baptism in suffering

Jesus also used the word baptise to describe the suffering he was going to subject himself to (Luke 12:50).

d) Baptism *by* the world *in* suffering. In response to the request of James and John, who asked to be seated on his right and on his left in his glory, Jesus asked if they could be baptised with the baptism he was to be baptised with. When they said yes, he confirmed that they would indeed suffer similarly (Mark 10:39). We know that James was put to death by Herod (Acts 12:2) and John was exiled to Patmos in his old age (Revelation 1:9).

Jesus told his disciples they were blessed if they were persecuted for his name's sake. They were in good company; all the Old Testament prophets provoked hatred. Besides, a great reward awaited them (Matthew 5:10-12). We must expect persecution for "a servant is not greater than his master" (John 15:20).

> All who wish to live godly in Christ Jesus will be persecuted.
>
> 2 Tim 3:12

When Paul felt the need to defend his apostleship to the Corinthian church he described to them the hardships he had endured because of his faith. By telling of his many afflictions he hoped to convince them that he was a true apostle, called by God (2 Corinthians 11:23-28).

When Jesus sent 72 disciples to evangelise the towns he was to visit, he said they were like lambs among wolves (Luke 10:3). Nevertheless, they came back rejoicing that even the demons submitted to them in his name. Jesus responded to their jubilation by saying: "I have given you authority ... to overcome all the power of the enemy; nothing will harm you". However, he counselled them to focus on their eternal reward rather than present successes (Luke 10:17-20).

Addressing his followers as his friends, Jesus encouraged them to have confidence in God. His aim was to dispel the anxieties and fears that

> You are worth more than many sparrows.
>
> Matthew 10:31

were likely to plague "lambs among wolves". **His first instruction** to them was *not to fear man but God* who had more power, knew them and highly valued them (Luke 12:4-7). **The second** was that they were not to prepare a defence when on trial for their faith. They should only resolve to confess their loyalty to Jesus. The Holy Spirit would teach them what to say at that time (Luke 12:8-12). **Thirdly**, Jesus told his disciples not to be anxious about money. They should differ from unbelievers in this respect because their Father cared for them. If they made his kingdom a priority all their needs would be met (Luke 12:22-34).

All suffering on earth originated in sin. It started when Adam and Eve decided to do the one thing they had been forbidden to do. God made sure that they would not be able to live forever in their sinful state (Genesis 3:22). For the Lord to have made garments of skin for them an animal had to die (Genesis 3:21). It pointed to the death of "the Lamb of God who takes away the sin of the world" (John 1:29). He was destined, before the foundation of the world, to buy us with his blood (1 Peter 1:18-20).

When someone is having a hard time it is not necessarily because of his/her own sin (John 9:2-3). The Lord called Job his servant and he said Job was blameless and upright (Job 1:8). Nevertheless he allowed satan to take away Job's possessions, children and health. At the end of his ordeal Job declared that, because of it, he had got to know God better.

> My ears had heard of you
> but now my eyes have seen you.
>
> Job 42:5

Of course it is also possible to bring suffering upon oneself through sin. We are warned not to cause ourselves grief through criminal acts or meddling in someone else's affairs (1 Peter 4:15). Sin can cause us to get sick or even die (1 Corinthians 11:29-30).

One of the ways in which we hurt ourselves is to give in to peer pressure. When pressurised one can become negligent and later regret the consequences of a bad decision. Paul prophesied about terrible times coming in the last days (2 Timothy 3:1). Daniel said that the antichrist will "wear out the saints of the Most High" (Daniel 7:25 KJV). When dealing with certain government departments or multi-corporations one could get the idea that these times have already arrived.

- Do you think being subjected to pressurised sales techniques is a form of persecution?

- Are you being persecuted for righteousness sake if your boss requests you to do something unethical?

Paul also wrote that deception and delusions would be characteristic of the last days (2 Thessalonians 2:9-12). Institutions funded with taxpayers' money propagate lies such as "evolution is a proven fact", "humans are born good but learn from society how to do evil", "Zionism is a threat to world peace" and many others. Governments and Hollywood indoctrinate the world that same sex marriages are "normal". One result of a humanistic mindset is that criminals often receive more sympathy than their victims.

When we suffer it is natural to ask: "Why?" In our bodies pain has the function of warning us that something is damaged. It can be regarded as our friend. We pity people who don't feel pain such as lepers. C.S. Lewis called pain "God's megaphone". He said it was God's way of shouting to get our attention. Parents inflict pain on their children to train them and God does the same to us (Hebrews 12:7-10).

God is more interested in our character than in our comfort.

Throughout the ages God's children have been persecuted for righteousness sake. Today is no exception; millions are cruelly discriminated against because of their faith. Peter encouraged Christians not to regard the "fiery ordeal" they were experiencing as something strange. When we endure insults and false accusations for Jesus' sake we are blessed (1 Peter 4:12-14). Paul believed that our hope is built up when we persevere (Romans 5:3-4). James goes so far as to say we should rejoice when we face trials because through them our character is formed (James 1:2-5).

It is important to remember that Jesus died for us while we were still sinners. It would be unreasonable for him to abandon us now. If we sin and become hard of hearing he may use circumstances to "shout at us". When we are in agony we can find comfort by reminding ourselves that "all things work together for good to those who love God" (Romans 8:28 KJV). Nothing can separate us from the love of God (Romans 8:38-39).

God uses the difficulties we go through to reach his elect who are not yet saved (2 Timothy 2:10). We are able to comfort others who find themselves in similar situations (2 Corinthians 1:4). The pain we now endure for a short while is not worth comparing to the glory that awaits us when we meet Jesus (Romans 8:18; 1 Peter 5:10).

We do not have control over all the experiences that come our way but we can manage our reaction to them. We may be tempted to blame fellow believers or even the Lord for our suffering. Instead, we are called to love God and one another (1 John 4:7-8).

6.

Laying on of hands

The words hand or hands occur in the King James version of the Bible more than one thousand five hundred times. *Hand* is mostly used in an idiomatic way to indicate *power* or *authority*. In some of the newer, less literal translations the word *hand* is not used in all these places. "In his hand" could for instance be replaced by "in his charge" and a "ring on his finger" could be substituted for "ring on his hand ".

One of the most obvious associations we have with our hands is that we **work** with them. Noah's father referred to the work of our hands (Genesis 5:29) and Jesus talked about putting one's hand to the plough (Luke 9:62). Paul reminded followers of Jesus that he and his colleagues earned a living by working with their hands . He commanded believers to do the same (1 Corinthians 4:12; 1 Thessalonians 4:11). There was work in the garden of Eden before Adam sinned (Genesis 2:8, 15).

> May the favor
> of the Lord our God
> rest on us;
> establish the work
> of our hands for us.
>
> Moses

Authors of the Bible described certain *acts of God* by referring to his hands. Creation is portrayed as the work of God's hands (Psalm 19:1). The Israelites were instructed to commemorate in perpetuity the event when the Lord led them out of Egypt with a mighty hand (Exodus 13:14). Nehemiah attributed the favour he obtained from the king to the fact that "the gracious hand" of his God was on him (Nehemiah 2:8). It is written of John the Baptist that the Lord's hand was with him (Luke 1:66). Jesus committed his spirit into his Father's hands (Luke 23:46). Threatened to stop preaching, the early church prayed: "Stretch out your hand to heal and perform signs and wonders through the name of your holy servant Jesus" (Acts 4:30).

Hands can be used to *do evil* to our fellow human beings. God told Cain that the ground received the blood of his brother from his hand (Genesis 4:11). Proverbs 6:16-19 mentions 7 things God hates. One of them is hands that shed innocent blood. Verses 3-4 of Psalm 24 describe the kind of person whom God welcomes into his presence. It is someone who has clean hands and a pure heart. Paul encouraged Christians not to use their bodies as tools of wickedness but to offer all the parts of their bodies as instruments of righteousness to God (Romans 6:13). Jesus repeatedly said that it would be better to cut off one's hand than allow it to cause one to sin (Matthew 5:30; 18:8).

We also use our hands to *do good*, such as lending someone a helping hand or stretching out a hand to a drowning person (Matthew 14:31). When Jacob met his brother after fourteen years he urged him saying "receive my present at my hand" (Genesis 33:10 KJV). When there was a famine in Judea the believers there were relieved by a gift which was sent "by the hands of Barnabas and Saul" (Acts 11:30 KJV). "Put your hand under my thigh" was an expression used by the patriarchs when they exacted a promise from someone (Genesis 24:2; 47:29).

To have something in one's hand is to have *power or control* over it. Potiphar put everything he owned in Joseph's hand (Genesis 39:4 KJV). The Lord told Noah and his sons that all the living creatures were given into their hands (Genesis 9:2). A ring on the hand can be an indication of status and authority (Genesis 41:42; Luke 15:22). The king's signet ring was used to seal documents (Esther 8:8). Today we still use our our hands to make our signatures. Putting someone's hands in chains is designed to deprive the person of power as in the case of Peter (Acts 12:6) and Paul (Acts 28:29).

Someone who has *power over a person's freedom of movement* is said to have the person in his/her hand. For example, Melchizedek gave praise to God Most High because he had delivered Abram's enemies into his hand (Genesis 14:20). Reuben rescued Joseph out of the hands of his brothers (Genesis 37:21). Jesus was betrayed into the hands of sinners who handed him over to the occupying power (Matthew 26:45; 27:2). Pilate, the resident governor, washed his hands in public to portray his alleged innocence of Jesus' blood (Matthew 27:24).

- Why does a man ask a woman's *hand* in marriage?

After Paul's conversion the church leaders in Jerusalem agreed to partner with him and Barnabas. They formalised this by giving them "the right hand of fellowship" (Galatians 2:9). Friends greet one another with a handshake. Business transactions between trusted parties are concluded by a handshake.

From the Bible at least five types of situations can be identified when hands were laid on people for their good:

a) Blessing. Jacob blessed his grand children by laying hands on them (Genesis 48:14) and Jesus blessed little children by doing the same (Matthew 19:13-15). Aaron lifted his hands toward the people and blessed them (Leviticus 9:22). Also, Jesus lifted up his hands and blessed his disciples while he ascended into heaven (Luke 24:50).

b) Healing. The most common way in which Jesus healed people was to lay hands on them (Mark 1:41). Notice that faith was necessary on the part of the receiver. Faith was present in the case of the woman with a bleeding problem (Mark 5:25-34) but mostly absent in Nazareth (Mark 6:5). He also said that those who believe in him would lay their hands on the sick and they will get well (Mark 16:18). Signs and wonders are said to have taken place through the hands of the apostles (Acts 14:3; 19:11). Sick believers are encouraged to call the elders to anoint them with oil and pray over them (James 5:14). It is implied that hands will be used and the sick person touched.

c) Baptism in the Holy Spirit. The book of Acts records five cases of people receiving the Holy Spirit. In three of these it happened through the laying on of hands: The people of Samaria (Acts 8:17), Saul (Acts 9:17) and the Ephesian disciples (Acts 19:6). The other two events occurred on the day of Pentecost and in the house of Cornelius respectively.

d) Impartation. Paul longed to go and *impart some spiritual gift* to help establish the church in Rome (Romans 1:11-12). The idea was that they would *catch* something from him. Something of his spirit would *rub off on them.* He encouraged Timothy not to neglect the gift he received by prophesy and the laying on of the elders' hands (1 Timothy 4:14). Paul also reminded Timothy to revive the gift which was in him through the laying on of his hands (2 Timothy 1:6). Whether these two verses refer to the same incident is not clear from the context. Moses and Elijah each imparted a spirit to his successor. In Moses' case it happened through the laying on of hands (2 Kings 2:15; Deuteronomy 34:9).

- Suppose a Christian lays hands on a demonised person. Do you think there is a risk that the evil spirit can be "caught" by the believer?

e) Ordination. The Lord instructed Moses to place his hands on Joshua so that some of the *majesty (authority)* which was on Moses would come on Joshua, causing the people to obey him (Numbers 27:18-23). The first deacons were also *commissioned* by the laying on of hands (Acts 6:6), as were the first missionaries to the gentile world (Acts 13:3). By cautioning Timothy not to lay hands on anyone hastily, Paul was saying that Timothy should be careful about whom he *ordained* as elders (1 Timothy 5:22). People are *authorised* and *empowered* when hands are laid on them. Jesus empowered his followers to exercise authority in his church (Matthew 16:19; 28:19-20; John 20:21-23).

7.

Resurrection of the dead

In Jesus' day the doctrines of Jewish religious leaders could be classified into two main groups. On the one hand were the Sadducees who denied the existence of angels, a spiritual world or life after death. The Pharisees, on the other hand, believed in them all (Acts 23:8). As far as *doctrine* was concerned Jesus agreed with the Pharisees, since their teachings were faithful to the books of Moses. He warned everyone, however, not to practise religion in the way the Pharisees did (Matthew 23:1-3).

> The Sadducees were sad, you see, since they did not believe in the resurrection of the dead.
>
> Matthew 22:23-32

John recorded how Jesus repeatedly promised those who believed in him that he would raise them up at *the last day* (John 6:39-40, 44, 54). Martha had a conversation with Jesus after the death of her brother Lazarus. She believed that Lazarus would "rise again in the resurrection at the last day" (John 11:24).

The patriarchs regarded their remains to be important enough to be entombed. Abraham bought a parcel of land which included a cave wherein he buried his wife Sarah. Later his sons buried him in the cave of Machpelah too. Jacob instructed his sons to carry his corpse from Egypt to that cave as well (Genesis 23:16-19; 25:9-10; 49:29-31). Joseph's bones also found their final resting place in the promised land after the Israelites had finally settled there (Joshua 24:32). These actions indicate that *they believed their bodies to have some significance after death.* The Egyptians took this concept to extremes by embalming corpses to last for millennia.

Old Testament Prophets announced that the bodies of those who had died would rise (Isaiah 26:19; Daniel 12:2). They said death would be done away with (Isaiah 25:8). Job believed that his redeemer would come to earth and that he would see him with his own eyes (Job 19:25-27).

In a debate with the Sadducees Jesus contrasted people of this age to people considered worthy of attaining to that age and the resurrection from the dead. In that age they could no longer die but would be like the angels (Luke 20:34-36).

Jesus referred to life after death as life in **the age to come**.

Matthew 12:32; Luke 18:29-30

Jesus predicted his own resurrection on several occasions but the disciples were slow to accept it. At the start of his preaching career he spoke of his body as a temple which, if destroyed, he would raise up in three days (John 2:19). After Peter had received the revelation from the Father that Jesus was the Messiah[†], Jesus began to explain to his apostles that he would die and rise again. Peter resisted the idea that God's Anointed should be executed. But Jesus reprimanded Peter for opposing God's plan of salvation (Matthew 16:21-23). From that time on he reminded his disciples on more than one occasion of his upcoming death and resurrection (Matthew 17:9, 22-23; 20:18-19).

After Jesus had risen an angel reminded the women who came to his grave of his promise to rise (Matthew 28:6). Jesus also berated the two disciples who were on the road to Emmaus for refusing to believe the prophets who had predicted his death and resurrection (Luke 24:25).

While the eleven were waiting for the outpouring of the Holy Spirit they chose Matthias to take the place of the apostle Judas Iscariot. In their minds his mission was to become a witness, with them, of the resurrection of Jesus (Acts 1:22). They wanted to tell the world of their Friend who had died and then rose with an immortal body.

[†]   The Hebrew word Messiah is Christos in Greek and Anointed in English.

On the day of Pentecost Peter quoted Psalm 16:8-11 to prove to the crowd that the Messiah was meant to rise from the dead (Acts 2:24-32). He spoke about it when he addressed the multitude that gathered after the lame man was healed at the gate Beautiful (Acts 3:26). This teaching greatly disturbed the priests (Acts 4:2). Their opposition did not prevent Peter from speaking out. He accused the high priest and rulers of crucifying Jesus (Acts 4:10). Furthermore, he openly disobeyed their order to stop spreading the good news of Jesus' resurrection (Acts 4:20, 33).

> Jesus' resurrection was the most important fact used by the apostles and evangelists to convert people.

The doctrine of the resurrection from the dead sets Christianity apart from all other religions. This theme occurs in almost all the sermons recorded in the Acts of the apostles. (Acts 5:29-32; 10:40-42; 13:30-37; 17:18; 17:31; 23:6; 24:14-15; 25:19; 26:23).

The reliability of books on history can be tested by asking:
a) Who wrote the original documents?
b) How long after the events were they written?
c) How close to the originals are the existing copies?

Lee Strobel, in his book THE CASE FOR CHRIST, answers these questions and many others about the truthfulness of the Bible. He shows that *no other historical fact of those days is documented as well* as the account of Jesus' resurrection.

a) Matthew and John, two of the authors who recorded the resurrection, were *eyewitnesses*. Mark was a close associate of Peter, who was an eyewitness. Luke wrote about what he had heard from eyewitnesses (Luke 1:1-2).

b) A papyrus fragment of a copy of John's gospel exists in the Rylands library England. It is dated to have been copied *before 150 AD*. Even critics of the Bible agree that John's gospel was written last. Matthew, Mark and Luke were therefore written *less that 120 years after the event.*

c) The Greek New Testament was translated into Syriac and Latin before 300 AD. In those three languages and others *over 24 000 manuscripts exist*, which are 99,5% in agreement. Compare this with Caesar's Gallic War, written about 50BC. There are 10 existing manuscripts, the oldest of which was copied 900 years after the event.

It is important to realise that Jesus' *body* was raised, not his spirit only, since *the tomb was empty* (Luke 24:3). He invited his disciples to look at his hands and feet and to touch him because, he said, "a ghost does not have flesh and bones" (Luke 24:39). He ate some fish, proving he was in a real body (Luke 24:42). Since flesh and blood cannot inherit the kingdom of God (1 Corinthians 15:50), we infer that Jesus had a new kind of body after he rose from the dead.

1 Corinthians 15, the whole chapter, deals with the resurrection of Christ and his followers.

First, Paul asserts that this teaching is an integral component of the Good News (1 Corinthians 15:1-4). *Believing that Jesus rose from the dead is an essential part of our faith.* It is doubtful that a person who does not believe in Jesus' resurrection can be saved (Romans 10:9-10). Those who believe in Christ for this life only, are of all people to be pitied most (1 Corinthians 15:19).

Secondly, Paul expands on the nature of the new bodies believers are to receive. They will be *imperishable, glorified, powerful and spiritual* (1 Corinthians 15:42-44). John said that when Jesus appears we shall be like him (1 John 3:2).

In the third place Paul associated our new bodies with the Second Coming. Believers who have died will rise first; then we who are alive will be *changed in the twinkling of an eye* (1 Corinthians 15:51-52). Paul linked our "adoption" to the "redemption of our bodies" (Romans 8:23). He had resolved to know Christ and the power of his resurrection (Philippians 3:8-11).

Since the time of Jesus' resurrection believers who die have immediate access to presence of God. Stephen committed his spirit to the Lord Jesus as he expired (Acts 7:59). Paul preferred to be "away from the body and at home with the Lord" and "to depart and be with Christ, which is better by far" (2 Corinthians 5:8; Philippians 1:23).

8.

Eternal judgement

The Bible does not leave us in any doubt about the fact that every human being has to die once and after that face "krisis", the Greek word for judgement (Hebrews 9:27). This word was normally used by Greeks in two settings namely law courts and games. In the Bible it speaks of two basic categories of judgements, namely for sins and for rewards.

Sins are judged by God on a continual basis during our lives on earth. Some sins bring their own judgement. For instance, if I lead a promiscuous life, I expose myself to infection of sexually transmitted diseases.

God has on occasion judged large groups of people for their sin. In the case of Noah's flood only eight people were saved. Just four escaped Sodom and Gomorrah and then one of them turned into a pillar of salt (Genesis 7:13; 19:12-26). Jesus spoke about Noah as well as Lot and his wife, warning us to be ready for his second coming which will be unexpected (Luke 17:26-28, 32). For believers there is the comfort that God will save us just as he saved Noah and Lot, and that we are not destined for his wrath (2 Peter 2:4-9; 1 Thessalonians 5:9).

We also receive earthly rewards for our deeds according to the principle of sowing and reaping. To anyone who left family or property for love of him, Jesus promised rewards in this life as well as in the next (Mark 10:29-30). This is in line with the way God dealt with Israel. Moses promised the Israelites God's blessings and warned of his curses in Deuteronomy 28. Paul decreed that those who *refuse to work,* should not be given food (2 Thessalonians 3:10). However, if someone is suffering, it is not necessarily because of sin (Job 2:3).

As Christians we ought to, on occasion, judge ourselves. That way we can avoid being judged and disciplined by the Lord. As a parent corrects a child by making the child feel pain, God disciplines us like a father (Hebrews 12:4-10). Sickness can be God's judgement to correct us. His aim is that we should escape being condemned with the world (1 Corinthians 11:28-32).

The rest of this lesson deals with **eternal judgement**. That is what we shall experience *after* death. Every child of God has already been judged for his/her sin. The wages of sin is death (Romans 6:23). However, Jesus died in our place. The sentence for sin has been passed. Jesus paid the penalty for those who put their faith in him. We do not come into judgement but have passed from death to life (John 5:24).

Death is better described by the word *separation* than the word *annihilation*. In Psalm 52:5 the wicked man is warned that God would uproot him from the land of the living. In Psalms 116:9 and 142:5 David talks about fellowship with God in the land of the living. Jesus and Paul both maintained that any form of life must include God (Luke 20:38; Acts 17:28). Eternal life is to know God (John 17:3). We were dead in our sins; our sins separated us from God (Ephesians 2:1; Isaiah 59:2). Only God gives life; to be separated from him is death.

Jesus suffered separation from his Father on our behalf. On the cross God was separated from God (Matthew 27:46). This is a mystery because Jesus never ceased to be God. The moment Jesus died the curtain in the temple was torn in two from top to bottom (Matthew 27:51). By that God indicated that human beings would from then on be allowed into his presence.

> Truly I tell you, today you will be with me in paradise.
>
> Luke 23:43

Most languages have a name for the *place of the dead*. In Greek it is *hades* and in Hebrew *sheol*. Some translators of the Bible into English have used the word *hell* for it. The Jews believed it to have two compartments. One part was known as *Abraham's Bosom* where the righteous resided. Those on the other side experienced eternal suffering. Jesus endorsed this belief in his story about Lazarus and the rich man (Luke 16:19-31). Today the righteous are no longer there because the price for their sin has been paid. Jesus promised the thief on the cross that he would be *with him* in paradise *that same day* (Luke 23:43).

The English word *hell* is also used to translate the Greek word *gehenna*, the place Jesus cautioned us to avoid, even if we had to cut off our right hand. It was derived from the word *ge-Hinnom*, Greek for the land of Hinnom, a place outside Jerusalem where refuse and corpses of criminals were burnt. Jesus' warning refers to the place which, in the book of Revelation, is called the lake of fire. Those whose names are not written in the book of life will be cast into it (Revelation 20:15).

The author of the book of Hebrews was convinced that the Old Testament heroes believed in an afterlife. They were looking forward to their rewards in the age to come (Hebrews 11:13-16). Jesus promised eternal rewards to his followers. The kingdom of heaven was to be theirs and he encouraged them to store up for themselves treasures in heaven (Matthew 5:3,10,12; 6:19-20). He promised a reward for a deed as small as offering a cup of water (Mark 9:41). Jesus spoke about rewards in the parable of the talents (Matthew 25:14-30) and the parable of the minas (Luke 19:12-27). In each of the letters to the seven churches in Revelation 2 and 3 the resurrected Jesus Christ promises an eternal reward to "the one who overcomes".

According to 2 Corinthians 5:10 "we must all appear before the judgement seat of Christ". This assertion is supported by John 5:22 and Acts 17:3. The apostles and Jesus spoke of crowns which his faithful followers would receive (1 Corinthians 9:25; 2 Timothy 4:8; James 1:12; 1 Peter 5:4; Revelation 2:10). Paul warned Christian ministers to build with gold, silver and costly stones, not wood, hay and straw since each person's work will be tested with fire (1 Corinthians 3:10-15).

On the final day of judgement earth and sky will flee away from the One sitting on the *great white throne.* He will judge the dead according to what they had done. The lost will share the lot of the devil and his angels. Everyone will not receive the same punishment (Revelation 20:11-15; Matthew 25:41; Luke 10:12; 12:47-48; 20:47).

"The Lord knows those who are his" (2 Timothy 2:19). We are not to judge whether another person is saved or not. (Matthew 7:1). In general we should accept his/her confession on face value. However, Jesus said: "Do not throw your pearls to pigs" (Matthew 7:6). To know whether someone is a pig we have to exercise some judgement. Someone who is blatantly disobedient to what God clearly commands, must not expect to be treated by us like a brother or a sister.

> When Jesus spoke about pigs he was not referring to the four-legged type.

Some believe that if they make a commitment to follow Jesus, it is impossible to renege on that decision. They think they can carry on sinning as long as they come back to God and ask for forgiveness. After all, David committed adultery and murder and was forgiven. Do such people realise how deeply David repented? Are they capable of repentance like that? They may not find it possible to believe God would forgive them; Judas did not.

> Restore to me the joy of **your** salvation.
> David

www.ingramcontent.com/pod-product-compliance
Lightning Source LLC
Chambersburg PA
CBHW061315140726
47998CB00006B/2401